Presented to

_____

On the occasion of

_____

From

_____

Date

_____

ISBN 1-57748-759-1

All Scripture quotations are taken from the Authorized King James Version of the Bible.

Published by Barbour Publishing, Inc., P.O. Box 719, Uhrichsville, Ohio 44683
http://www.barbourbooks.com

Member of the
Evangelical Christian
Publishers Association

Printed in China.

YOU HAVE MY
WORD

175 Promises of God

BARBOUR
PUBLISHING, INC..

For God so loved the world, that he gave his only begotten Son, that whosoever believeth in him should not perish, but have everlasting life. JOHN 3:16

∽

To him give all the prophets witness, that through his name whosoever believeth in him shall receive remission of sins. ACTS 10:43

∽

He that believeth on him is not condemned: but he that believeth not is condemned already, because he hath not believed in the name of the only begotten Son of God. JOHN 3:18

∽

Jesus said unto him, If thou canst believe, all things are possible to him that believeth. MARK 9:23

∽

I am come a light into the world, that whosoever believeth on me should not abide in darkness. JOHN 12:46

*Cast
thy
burden
upon
the
Lord*

God is our refuge and strength, a very present help in trouble.

Therefore will not we fear, though the earth be removed, and though the mountains be carried into the midst of the sea;

Though the waters thereof roar and be troubled, though the mountains shake with the swelling thereof.

PSALM 46:1–3

Though I walk in the midst of trouble, thou wilt revive me: thou shalt stretch forth thine hand against the wrath of mine enemies, and thy right hand shall save me.

PSALM 138:7

The LORD is my rock, and my fortress, and my deliverer; my God, my strength, in whom I will trust; my buckler, and the horn of my salvation, and my high tower.

PSALM 18:2

Cast thy burden upon the LORD, and he shall sustain thee: he shall never suffer the righteous to be moved.

PSALM 55:22

A merry heart doeth good like a medicine: but a broken spirit drieth the bones.   PROVERBS 17:22

~

Let your conversation be without covetousness; and be content with such things as ye have: for he hath said, I will never leave thee, nor forsake thee.   HEBREWS 13:5

~

All the days of the afflicted are evil: but he that is of a merry heart hath a continual feast.   PROVERBS 15:15

~

A sound heart is the life of the flesh: but envy the rottenness of the bones.   PROVERBS 14:30

~

But godliness with contentment is great gain.
                              1 TIMOTHY 6:6

~

Whoso trusteth in the LORD, happy is he.
                              PROVERBS 16:20

A sound heart is the life of the flesh

Eternal Life

Though he were dead, yet shall he live

Verily, verily, I say unto you, He that believeth on me hath everlasting life.   JOHN 6:47

∽

Jesus said unto her, I am the resurrection, and the life: he that believeth in me, though he were dead, yet shall he live:

And whosoever liveth and believeth in me shall never die. Believest thou this?   JOHN 11:25–26

∽

Behold, I show you a mystery; We shall not all sleep, but we shall all be changed,

In a moment, in the twinkling of an eye, at the last trump: for the trumpet shall sound, and the dead shall be raised incorruptible, and we shall be changed.

For this corruptible must put on incorruption, and this mortal must put on immortality.

So when this corruptible shall have put on incorruption, and this mortal shall have put on immortality, then shall be brought to pass the saying that is written, Death is swallowed up in victory.

1 CORINTHIANS 15:51–54

And this is the promise that he hath promised us, even eternal life.   1 JOHN 2:25

∾

Marvel not at this: for the hour is coming, in the which all that are in the graves shall hear his voice,

And shall come forth; they that have done good, unto the resurrection of life; and they that have done evil, unto the resurrection of damnation.   JOHN 5:28–29

∾

And this is the record, that God hath given to us eternal life, and this life is in his Son.   1 JOHN 5:11

∾

These things have I written unto you that believe on the name of the Son of God; that ye may know that ye have eternal life, and that ye may believe on the name of the Son of God.   1 JOHN 5:13

∾

For the wages of sin is death; but the gift of God is eternal life through Jesus Christ our Lord.

        ROMANS 6:23

The gift of God is eternal life

Stand fast in the faith

Now faith is the substance of things hoped for, the evidence of things not seen.   HEBREWS 11:1

Watch ye, stand fast in the faith, quit you like men, be strong.   1 CORINTHIANS 16:13

For by grace are ye saved through faith; and that not of yourselves: it is the gift of God.   EPHESIANS 2:8

If any of you lack wisdom, let him ask of God, that giveth to all men liberally, and upbraideth not; and it shall be given him.

But let him ask in faith, nothing wavering. For he that wavereth is like a wave of the sea driven with the wind and tossed.   JAMES 1:5–6

As ye have therefore received Christ Jesus the Lord, so walk ye in him:

Rooted and built up in him, and stablished in the faith, as ye have been taught, abounding therein with thanksgiving.   COLOSSIANS 2:6–7

For ye are all the children of God by faith in Christ Jesus.
GALATIANS 3:26

∾

And Jesus answering saith unto them, Have faith in God.

For verily I say unto you, That whosoever shall say unto this mountain, Be thou removed, and be thou cast into the sea; and shall not doubt in his heart, but shall believe that those things which he saith shall come to pass; he shall have whatsoever he saith.
MARK 11:22–23

∾

But the fruit of the Spirit is love, joy, peace, longsuffering, gentleness, goodness, faith,

Meekness, temperance: against such there is no law.
GALATIANS 5:22–23

∾

For we walk by faith, not by sight. 2 CORINTHIANS 5:7

∾

But without faith it is impossible to please him; for he that cometh to God must believe that he is, and that he is a rewarder of them that diligently seek him.

HEBREWS 11:6

Forgiveness

Forgive, and ye shall be forgiven

But I say unto you, Love your enemies, bless them that curse you, do good to them that hate you, and pray for them which despitefully use you, and persecute you;

That ye may be the children of your Father which is in heaven: for he maketh his sun to rise on the evil and on the good, and sendeth rain on the just and on the unjust. MATTHEW 5:44–45

But love ye your enemies, and do good, and lend, hoping for nothing again; and your reward shall be great, and ye shall be the children of the Highest: for he is kind unto the unthankful and to the evil.

Be ye therefore merciful, as your Father also is merciful.

Judge not, and ye shall not be judged: condemn not, and ye shall not be condemned: forgive, and ye shall be forgiven. LUKE 6:35–37

For if ye forgive men their trespasses, your heavenly Father will also forgive you. MATTHEW 6:14

If we confess our sins, he is faithful and just to forgive us our sins. 1 JOHN 1:9

And he shall be like a tree planted by the rivers of water, that bringeth forth his fruit in his season; his leaf also shall not wither; and whatsoever he doeth shall prosper.

PSALM 1:3

Therefore they shall come and sing in the height of Zion, and shall flow together to the goodness of the LORD, for wheat, and for wine, and for oil, and for the young of the flock and of the herd: and their soul shall be as a watered garden; and they shall not sorrow any more at all.

JEREMIAH 31:12

I will be as the dew unto Israel: he shall grow as the lily, and cast forth his roots as Lebanon.   HOSEA 14:5

For if these things be in you, and abound, they make you that ye shall neither be barren nor unfruitful in the knowledge of our Lord Jesus Christ.   2 PETER 1:8

Herein is my Father glorified, that ye bear much fruit; so shall ye be my disciples.   JOHN 15:8

Ye bear much fruit; so shall ye be my disciples

God's Faithfulness

He hath remembered his covenant for ever, the word which he commanded to a thousand generations.

PSALM 105:8

Let us hold fast the profession of our faith without wavering; (for he is faithful that promised). HEBREWS 10:23

Know therefore that the LORD thy God, he is God, the faithful God, which keepeth covenant and mercy with them that love him and keep his commandments to a thousand generations. DEUTERONOMY 7:9

(For the LORD thy God is a merciful God;) he will not forsake thee, neither destroy thee, nor forget the covenant of thy fathers which he sware unto them.

DEUTERONOMY 4:31

Blessed be the LORD, that hath given rest unto his people Israel, according to all that he promised: there hath not failed one word of all his good promise. 1 KINGS 8:56

14

God is not a man, that he should lie; neither the son of man, that he should repent: hath he said, and shall he not do it? or hath he spoken, and shall he not make it good?

NUMBERS 23:19

∽

If we believe not, yet he abideth faithful: he cannot deny himself.

2 TIMOTHY 2:13

∽

The Lord is not slack concerning his promise, as some men count slackness; but is longsuffering to us-ward.

2 PETER 3:9

∽

And they that know thy name will put their trust in thee: for thou, LORD, hast not forsaken them that seek thee.

PSALM 9:10

∽

My covenant will I not break, nor alter the thing that is gone out of my lips.

PSALM 89:34

∽

Faithful is he that calleth you, who also will do it.

1 THESSALONIANS 5:24

My covenant will I not break

15

God's Love

We love him, because he first loved us

For the Father himself loveth you, because ye have loved me, and have believed that I came out from God.

JOHN 16:27

∽

We love him, because he first loved us.   1 JOHN 4:19

∽

For God so loved the world, that he gave his only begotten Son, that whosoever believeth in him should not perish, but have everlasting life.   JOHN 3:16

∽

The LORD openeth the eyes of the blind: the LORD raiseth them that are bowed down: the LORD loveth the righteous.

PSALM 146:8

∽

For as a young man marrieth a virgin, so shall thy sons marry thee: and as the bridegroom rejoiceth over the bride, so shall thy God rejoice over thee.

ISAIAH 62:5

Herein is love, not that we loved God, but that he loved us, and sent his Son to be the propitiation for our sins.

1 JOHN 4:10

I will heal their backsliding, I will love them freely: for mine anger is turned away from him.　　HOSEA 14:4

And I have declared unto them thy name, and will declare it: that the love wherewith thou hast loved me may be in them, and I in them.　　JOHN 17:26

But God, who is rich in mercy, for his great love wherewith he loved us,

Even when we were dead in sins, hath quickened us together with Christ, (by grace ye are saved;)

And hath raised us up together, and made us sit together in heavenly places in Christ Jesus:

That in the ages to come he might show the exceeding riches of his grace in his kindness toward us through Christ Jesus.　　EPHESIANS 2:4–7

Growth in Grace

And beside this, giving all diligence, add to your faith virtue; and to virtue knowledge.   2 PETER 1:5

∽

And this I pray, that your love may abound yet more and more in knowledge and in all judgment.

PHILIPPIANS 1:9

∽

Being filled with the fruits of righteousness, which are by Jesus Christ, unto the glory and praise of God.

PHILIPPIANS 1:11

∽

The righteous also shall hold on his way, and he that hath clean hands shall be stronger and stronger.   JOB 17:9

∽

Furthermore then we beseech you, brethren, and exhort you by the Lord Jesus, that as ye have received of us how ye ought to walk and to please God, so ye would abound more and more.   1 THESSALONIANS 4:1

But we all, with open face beholding as in a glass the glory of the Lord, are changed into the same image from glory to glory, even as by the Spirit of the Lord.

2 CORINTHIANS 3:18

~~

The LORD will perfect that which concerneth me: thy mercy, O LORD, endureth for ever: forsake not the works of thine own hands.   PSALM 138:8

~~

Which is come unto you, as it is in all the world; and bringeth forth fruit, as it doth also in you, since the day ye heard of it, and knew the grace of God in truth.

COLOSSIANS 1:6

~~

We are bound to thank God always for you, brethren, as it is meet, because that your faith groweth exceedingly, and the charity of every one of you all toward each other aboundeth.   2 THESSALONIANS 1:3

~~

He which hath begun a good work in you will perform it until the day of Jesus Christ.   PHILIPPIANS 1:6

Changed into the same image from glory to glory

Guidance

And thine ears shall hear a word behind thee, saying, This is the way, walk ye in it, when ye turn to the right hand, and when ye turn to the left. ISAIAH 30:21

For this God is our God for ever and ever: he will be our guide even unto death. PSALM 48:14

A man's heart deviseth his way: but the LORD directeth his steps. PROVERBS 16:9

The steps of a good man are ordered by the LORD: and he delighteth in his way. PSALM 37:23

The righteousness of the perfect shall direct his way: but the wicked shall fall by his own wickedness.

PROVERBS 11:5

For his God doth instruct him to discretion, and doth teach him. ISAIAH 28:26

And I will bring the blind by a way that they knew not; I will lead them in the paths that they have not known: I will make darkness light before them, and crooked things straight. These things will I do unto them, and not forsake them.   ISAIAH 42:16

∽

In all thy ways acknowledge him, and he shall direct thy paths.   PROVERBS 3:6

∽

Nevertheless I am continually with thee: thou hast holden me by my right hand.

Thou shalt guide me with thy counsel, and afterward receive me to glory.   PSALM 73:23–24

∽

I will instruct thee and teach thee in the way which thou shalt go: I will guide thee with mine eye.   PSALM 32:8

∽

Lead me in thy truth, and teach me: for thou art the God of my salvation; on thee do I wait all the day.

PSALM 25:5

Lead me in thy truth, and teach me

21

Help in Troubles

The Lord is good, a strong hold in the day of trouble

Behold, God will not cast away a perfect man, neither will he help the evil doers:

Till he fill thy mouth with laughing, and thy lips with rejoicing. JOB 8:20–21

∽

These things I have spoken unto you, that in me ye might have peace. In the world ye shall have tribulation: but be of good cheer; I have overcome the world.

JOHN 16:33

∽

The LORD is good, a strong hold in the day of trouble; and he knoweth them that trust in him. NAHUM 1:7

∽

But I am poor and needy; yet the LORD thinketh upon me: thou art my help and my deliverer. PSALM 40:17

∽

Many are the afflictions of the righteous: but the LORD delivereth him out of them all. PSALM 34:19

There shall no evil befall thee, neither shall any plague come nigh thy dwelling.

For he shall give his angels charge over thee, to keep thee in all thy ways. PSALM 91:10–11

⁓

Thou art my hiding place; thou shalt preserve me from trouble; thou shalt compass me about with songs of deliverance. PSALM 32:7

⁓

Though he fall, he shall not be utterly cast down: for the LORD upholdeth him with his hand. PSALM 37:24

⁓

But the salvation of the righteous is of the LORD: he is their strength in the time of trouble. PSALM 37:39

⁓

Thou, which hast shewed me great and sore troubles, shalt quicken me again, and shalt bring me up again from the depths of the earth. PSALM 71:20

For he shall give his angels charge over thee

Which
is
Christ
in you,
the
hope of
glory

Why art thou cast down, O my soul? and why art thou disquieted within me? hope thou in God: for I shall yet praise him, who is the health of my countenance, and my God. PSALM 42:11

. . .which is Christ in you, the hope of glory.
COLOSSIANS 1:27

Be of good courage, and he shall strengthen your heart, all ye that hope in the LORD. PSALM 31:24

Who by him do believe in God, that raised him up from the dead, and gave him glory; that your faith and hope might be in God. 1 PETER 1:21

Blessed be the God and Father of our Lord Jesus Christ, which according to his abundant mercy hath begotten us again unto a lively hope by the resurrection of Jesus Christ from the dead. 1 PETER 1:3

For the hope which is laid up for you in heaven, whereof ye heard before in the word of the truth of the gospel.

COLOSSIANS 1:5

∽

For thou art my hope, O Lord GOD: thou art my trust from my youth.

PSALM 71:5

∽

Wherefore gird up the loins of your mind, be sober, and hope to the end for the grace that is to be brought unto you at the revelation of Jesus Christ.

1 PETER 1:13

∽

The wicked is driven away in his wickedness: but the righteous hath hope in his death.

PROVERBS 14:32

∽

And now, Lord, what wait I for? my hope is in thee.

PSALM 39:7

∽

Be not a terror unto me: thou art my hope in the day of evil.

JEREMIAH 17:17

They that sow in tears shall reap in joy

For ye shall go out with joy, and be led forth with peace: the mountains and the hills shall break forth before you into singing, and all the trees of the field shall clap their hands.   ISAIAH 55:12

They that sow in tears shall reap in joy.

He that goeth forth and weepeth, bearing precious seed, shall doubtless come again with rejoicing, bringing his sheaves with him.   PSALM 126:5–6

Blessed is the people that know the joyful sound: they shall walk, O LORD, in the light of thy countenance.

In thy name shall they rejoice all the day: in thy righteousness shall they be exalted.   PSALM 89:15–16

For then shalt thou have thy delight in the Almighty, and shalt lift up thy face unto God.   JOB 22:26

Yet I will rejoice in the LORD, I will joy in the God of my salvation.   HABAKKUK 3:18

The voice of rejoicing and salvation is in the tabernacles of the righteous: the right hand of the LORD doeth valiantly. PSALM 118:15

∿

These things I have spoken unto you, that my joy might remain in you, and that your joy might be full.

JOHN 15:11

∿

Light is sown for the righteous, and gladness for the upright in heart.

Rejoice in the LORD, ye righteous; and give thanks at the remembrance of his holiness. PSALM 97:11–12

∿

Whom having not seen, ye love; in whom, though now ye see him not, yet believing, ye rejoice with joy unspeakable and full of glory. 1 PETER 1:8

∿

And ye now therefore have sorrow: but I will see you again, and your heart shall rejoice, and your joy no man taketh from you. JOHN 16:22

Joy

I will see you again, and your heart shall rejoice

Long Life

With long life will I satisfy him

And even to your old age I am he; and even to hoar hairs will I carry you: I have made, and I will bear; even I will carry, and will deliver you.　　　ISAIAH 46:4

My son, forget not my law; but let thine heart keep my commandments:

For length of days, and long life, and peace, shall they add to thee.　　　PROVERBS 3:1–2

Ye shall walk in all the ways which the LORD your God hath commanded you, that ye may live, and that it may be well with you, and that ye may prolong your days in the land ye shall possess.　　　DEUTERONOMY 5:33

With long life will I satisfy him, and show him my salvation.　　　PSALM 91:16

For by me thy days shall be multiplied, and the years of thy life shall be increased.　　　PROVERBS 9:11

A new commandment I give unto you, That ye love one another; as I have loved you, that ye also love one another.

By this shall all men know that ye are my disciples, if ye have love one to another.   JOHN 13:34–35

∽

Let love be without dissimulation. Abhor that which is evil; cleave to that which is good.

Be kindly affectioned one to another with brotherly love; in honour preferring one another.

ROMANS 12:9–10

∽

He that loveth his brother abideth in the light, and there is none occasion of stumbling in him.

1 JOHN 2:10

∽

Beloved, let us love one another: for love is of God; and every one that loveth is born of God, and knoweth God.

He that loveth not knoweth not God; for God is love.
1 JOHN 4:7–8

He that loveth his brother abideth in the light

The Lord pitieth them that fear him

And therefore will the LORD wait, that he may be gracious unto you, and therefore will he be exalted, that he may have mercy upon you: for the LORD is a God of judgment: blessed are all they that wait for him.

ISAIAH 30:18

Know therefore that God exacteth of thee less than thine iniquity deserveth. JOB 11:6

And I will have mercy upon her that had not obtained mercy; and I will say to them which were not my people, Thou art my people; and they shall say, Thou art my God. HOSEA 2:23

But the mercy of the LORD is from everlasting to everlasting upon them that fear him, and his righteousness unto children's children. PSALM 103:17

Like as a father pitieth his children, so the LORD pitieth them that fear him. PSALM 103:13

And he said, I will make all my goodness pass before thee, and I will proclaim the name of the LORD before thee; and will be gracious to whom I will be gracious, and will show mercy on whom I will show mercy.

EXODUS 33:19

∽

For in my wrath I smote thee, but in my favour have I had mercy on thee. ISAIAH 60:10

∽

For my name's sake will I defer mine anger, and for my praise will I refrain for thee, that I cut thee not off.

ISAIAH 48:9

∽

Thou in thy mercy hast led forth the people which thou hast redeemed: thou hast guided them in thy strength unto thy holy habitation. EXODUS 15:13

∽

O give thanks unto the LORD; for he is good; for his mercy endureth for ever. 1 CHRONICLES 16:34

Mercy

In my favour have I had mercy on thee

Patience

The trying of your faith worketh patience

My brethren, count it all joy when ye fall into divers temptations;

Knowing this, that the trying of your faith worketh patience.

But let patience have her perfect work, that ye may be perfect and entire, wanting nothing.   JAMES 1:2–4

∽

And let us not be weary in well doing: for in due season we shall reap, if we faint not.   GALATIANS 6:9

∽

But he that shall endure unto the end, the same shall be saved.   MATTHEW 24:13

∽

That ye be not slothful, but followers of them who through faith and patience inherit the promises.

HEBREWS 6:12

∽

For ye have need of patience, that, after ye have done the will of God, ye might receive the promise.

HEBREWS 10:36

And let the peace of God rule in your hearts, to the which also ye are called in one body; and be ye thankful.

COLOSSIANS 3:15

∽

I will hear what God the LORD will speak: for he will speak peace unto his people, and to his saints.

PSALM 85:8

∽

And the peace of God, which passeth all understanding, shall keep your hearts and minds through Christ Jesus.

PHILIPPIANS 4:7

∽

Thy faith hath saved thee; go in peace. LUKE 7:50

∽

Peace I leave with you, my peace I give unto you: not as the world giveth, give I unto you. Let not your heart be troubled, neither let it be afraid. JOHN 14:27

∽

Mark the perfect man, and behold the upright: for the end of that man is peace. PSALM 37:37

He will answer thee

Ask, and it shall be given you; seek, and ye shall find; knock, and it shall be opened unto you:

For every one that asketh receiveth; and he that seeketh findeth; and to him that knocketh it shall be opened.

MATTHEW 7:7–8

And all things, whatsoever ye shall ask in prayer, believing, ye shall receive. MATTHEW 21:22

He will be very gracious unto thee at the voice of thy cry; when he shall hear it, he will answer thee.

ISAIAH 30:19

Then shall ye call upon me, and ye shall go and pray unto me, and I will hearken unto you. JEREMIAH 29:12

And this is the confidence that we have in him, that, if we ask any thing according to his will, he heareth us:

And if we know that he hear us, whatsoever we ask, we know that we have the petitions that we desired of him.

1 JOHN 5:14–15

And whatsoever ye shall ask in my name, that will I do, that the Father may be glorified in the Son.

If ye shall ask any thing in my name, I will do it.

JOHN 14:13–14

◦

And it shall come to pass, that before they call, I will answer; and while they are yet speaking, I will hear.

ISAIAH 65:24

◦

Thou shalt make thy prayer unto him, and he shall hear thee.

JOB 22:27

◦

Confess your faults one to another, and pray one for another, that ye may be healed. The effectual fervent prayer of a righteous man availeth much.   JAMES 5:16

◦

Evening, and morning, and at noon, will I pray, and cry aloud: and he shall hear my voice.   PSALM 55:17

Effectual fervent prayer. . . availeth much

Ye must be born again

Therefore if any man be in Christ, he is a new creature: old things are passed away; behold, all things are become new. 2 CORINTHIANS 5:17

⚭

But not as the offence, so also is the free gift. For if through the offence of one many be dead, much more the grace of God, and the gift by grace, which is by one man, Jesus Christ, hath abounded unto many. ROMANS 5:15

⚭

Jesus answered and said unto him, Verily, verily, I say unto thee, Except a man be born again, he cannot see the kingdom of God.

Nicodemus saith unto him, How can a man be born when he is old? can he enter the second time into his mother's womb, and be born?

Jesus answered, Verily, verily, I say unto thee, Except a man be born of water and of the Spirit, he cannot enter into the kingdom of God.

That which is born of the flesh is flesh; and that which is born of the Spirit is spirit.

Marvel not that I said unto thee, Ye must be born again. JOHN 3:3–7

For he hath made him to be sin for us, who knew no sin; that we might be made the righteousness of God in him.

2 CORINTHIANS 5:21

∽

My little children, these things write I unto you, that ye sin not. And if any man sin, we have an advocate with the Father, Jesus Christ the righteous:

And he is the propitiation for our sins: and not for ours only, but also for the sins of the whole world.

1 JOHN 2:1–2

∽

For this is good and acceptable in the sight of God our Saviour;

Who will have all men to be saved, and to come unto the knowledge of the truth.   1 TIMOTHY 2:3–4

∽

This is a faithful saying and worthy of all acceptation.

For therefore we both labour and suffer reproach, because we trust in the living God, who is the Saviour of all men, specially of those that believe.

1 TIMOTHY 4:9-10

God, who is the Saviour of all men

37

Sin, Freedom from

He that is dead is freed from sin

To him give all the prophets witness, that through his name whosoever believeth in him shall receive remission of sins.

ACTS 10:43

◦

Knowing this, that our old man is crucified with him, that the body of sin might be destroyed, that henceforth we should not serve sin.

For he that is dead is freed from sin.

ROMANS 6:6–7

◦

For sin shall not have dominion over you: for ye are not under the law, but under grace.   ROMANS 6:14

◦

What shall we say then? Shall we continue in sin, that grace may abound?

God forbid. How shall we, that are dead to sin, live any longer therein?   ROMANS 6:1–2

◦

Likewise reckon ye also yourselves to be dead indeed unto sin, but alive unto God through Jesus Christ our Lord.

ROMANS 6:11

And she shall bring forth a son, and thou shalt call his name JESUS: for he shall save his people from their sins.
MATTHEW 1:21

~

And if any man sin, we have an advocate with the Father, Jesus Christ the righteous:

And he is the propitiation for our sins: and not for ours only, but also for the sins of the whole world.
1 JOHN 2:1–2

~

In whom we have redemption through his blood, the forgiveness of sins, according to the riches of his grace.
EPHESIANS 1:7

~

But he was wounded for our transgressions, he was bruised for our iniquities: the chastisement of our peace was upon him; and with his stripes we are healed.

All we like sheep have gone astray; we have turned every one to his own way; and the LORD hath laid on him the iniquity of us all.
ISAIAH 53:5–6

He shall save his people from their sins

Wisdom

For God giveth to a man... wisdom

If any of you lack wisdom, let him ask of God, that giveth to all men liberally, and upbraideth not; and it shall be given him.   JAMES 1:5

∽

And he will teach us of his ways, and we will walk in his paths.   ISAIAH 2:3

∽

I will instruct thee and teach thee in the way which thou shalt go: I will guide thee with mine eye.

PSALM 32:8

∽

For God giveth to a man that is good in his sight wisdom, and knowledge, and joy.   ECCLESIASTES 2:26

∽

And we know that the Son of God is come, and hath given us an understanding, that we may know him that is true, and we are in him that is true, even in his Son Jesus Christ. This is the true God, and eternal life.

1 JOHN 5:20